Copyright © 2019 Gerald Rennett

All rights reserved. No part of this book may be reproduced, stored in a retrieval system, or transmitted in any form or by any means without the express written permission of the publisher except for the use of brief quotations in a book review.

A Few Words Of Introduction

Welcome on board the Rutland Belle! Rutland Water's iconic pleasure boat! As you settle down in one of our comfortable salon seats or, if the weather is fine, take your place on the upper deck, you will hear Captain Matt welcome you on board. We will cast off from Whitwell Harbour Pontoon and start the commentary on the places of interest that we pass, or in one case, moor at, during our forty-five minute round-trip cruise. This year, 2022, we've included on-line ticketing as part of our brand-new website which has been incredibly popular although you can, of course, still buy tickets down at the boat!

It is only possible to briefly sketch a quick picture in our regular commentary and many of our visitors request more information. This little guide is intended to fill in some of those gaps and give you an insight into the background and history which surrounds one of Europe's largest man-made reservoirs – Rutland Water. Much has changed since it was first released in 2019 and so this revised and updated version contains even more useful information for planning your visit to Rutland Water and the Belle!

So, have a great trip today and I hope you enjoy reading this guide as much as I enjoyed writing it!

Gerald Rennett
Burley
May 2022

Contents

Safety Announcements
Rutland Water
Whitwell
Whitwell Harbour
Sykes Lane – Monument & Beach
The Dam
Empingham – A Model Village
Normanton Park and Village
Normanton Church
South Shore – Fishing & Sailing
North Shore – Rutland Fly Fishing Adventures

South Arm – Nature Reserve
Hambleton Peninsula and The Hambletons
The North Arm and Burley-on-the-Hill
The Rutland OspreysThe Rutland Sea Dragon – Ancient History is brought to life!
Barnsdale Gardens – It's In The Genes!
Rocks By Rail – The Living Ironstone Museum
2021 – New Year New Look
The Rutland Belle, Class V Passenger Vessel
Multum In Parvo – Rutland in brief
Acknowledgements

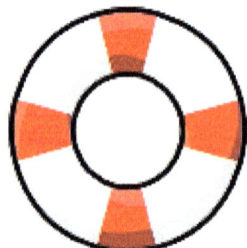

"There is certainly no circumstance of landscape more interesting or beautiful than water and there can be no person so void of taste as not to feel the necessity of improving the valley at Normanton by enlarging the river, yet this is a subject attended with some difficulty and requires more management than may at first be conceived; for though it might be possible to make such a dam or head as would convert the whole valley into one vast lake, yet the expense of such a bank, and the waste of so much valuable land, is more than I would dare to advise…"

Humphrey Repton, 1797

Safety Announcements

Before we cast off, we are required by Maritime Law to issue the following Safety Announcements so please listen carefully to the Captain as he goes through them:

 In the unlikely event of an emergency you will hear the general emergency signal, which is seven short blasts on the ship's horn, followed by one long blast.

 Upon hearing this signal, please remain calm, stay where you are and follow the instructions of the crew.

 For your information, life-rings and life rafts are located on the upper decks and access to them is from the doors located mid-ships, port and starboard.

 Due to the intricate nature of the ship's communication systems, the use of mobile phones is not permitted on board. We would therefore ask you to turn them off for the duration of the cruise.

Rutland Water

Rutland Water, owned by Anglian Water, was officially opened in 1976, ironically one of the UK's driest years. The 1976 heatwave led to the second hottest summer average temperature in the UK since records began, with the country suffering a severe drought as a result. The reservoir was first conceived in the 1960s when Anglian Water Authority, as it was then known, forecast a rise in demand for water and, in order to meet that demand, decided to build a storage supply reservoir. Nearly ninety sites in the East Midlands region were considered before Rutland was finally decided upon mainly for the following two reasons. The Gwash Valley near Empingham has a very heavy clay bottom which is good for water retention and the geography of the valley meant that the required dam would not need to be overly large in relation to the amount of water that could be stored behind it.

Work was started on the construction of the dam in 1970 and took five years to complete. It then took a further three years to fill with water and by 1978 Rutland Water became operational. The resultant reservoir flooded seven square kilometres of the Gwash Valley and also the side valley that led to Oakham. Of the three Hambleton Hamlets, Nether Hambleton was completely demolished and Middle Hambleton partially demolished and their wells plugged. Today only Upper Hambleton survives and is now known simply as Hambleton. Hambleton Hall, a former Hunting Box built by Walter Marshall survived and today is the well-known Hambleton Hall Country House Hotel.

Photo courtesy of Rob Waddington, Lakeside B&B and Rutland Flyfishing Adventures (full details on photo credits page)

The area of land, over which the former Upper Hambleton presides, is now known as Hambleton Peninsula.

The reservoir is still fed by the Gwash, although its downstream flow below the dam is maintained. Most of the stored water is actually extracted from the River Nene, at Wansford south of Stamford and the River Welland at Tinwell through a network of underground pipes, usually over the winter period when there is a plentiful supply of water, and the reservoir is usually full by May. The extraction points explain the slight incongruity of the drinking water reservoir being owned by Anglian Water although Rutland County itself is actually served by Severn Trent. Rutland Water supplies Peterborough and its surrounds as well as Milton Keynes, Northampton and Lincoln areas.

Rutland Water has a surface area of 3100 acres, a perimeter of roughly 24 miles and a length of approximately 5 miles. When full, it contains 27 billion gallons of drinking water – approximately 124 billion litres. The pipelines supplying it from the Rivers Nene and Welland total 12 miles. It is stocked with 130,000 brown and rainbow trout and is also home to the Rutland Sailing Club which is one of the largest in the country with over a thousand members. The Nature Reserve covers 9 miles of shoreline, with many shallow lagoons and hides.

The late Geoff Hamilton, of Gardeners' World fame with two 'Parisiennes'

Whitwell

Whitwell, in common with other villages of the same name, derives its name from the Old English, *'hwit'* (white) + *'well'* (spring or stream). In Whitwell's case, the spring rises in the hillside behind the church. Following the Norman Conquest it was surveyed for the Domesday Book which valued the estate at 40 shillings with ten villagers / smallholders. The Noel family of nearby Exton Hall, Earls of Gainsborough, acquired the manor of Whitwell in the seventeenth century. They were staunch Royalists and during the English Civil War, Baptist Noel, 3rd Viscount Campden led a cavalry troop known as the 'Campdeners' across Rutland and beyond, even being involved in action at the Burghley House siege in Stamford. By the nineteenth century, Whitwell's population was around eighty strong. Following the two World Wars, Whitwell remained an estate village with most residents and farmers paying rent to the Gainsborough Estate (Exton). Today it is mainly populated by owner-occupiers and with a population of around fifty.

'Parisiens' celebrate the twinning with Rutland Morris Men. Julie Healy second from left.

Whitwell is probably most well-known locally, for its claim to be twinned with Paris. Stories vary about this but it is agreed that it dates back to the new owners of the Noel Arms, Whitwell's pub (now known as 'The Noel'), Sam and Julie Healey, who bought it in 1979. Under their management, the pub became the centre of the village community and the story that I've been told, by a long-standing local, is that Sam's customers light-heartedly compared the Noel's outside privies with a Parisian 'Pissoir'.

Picking up on this theme, two villagers wrote to the then Mayor of Paris, Jacques Chirac, later to become the French President, to inform him that they intended to link Whitwell with Paris and inviting him to the ceremony. The letter is worth quoting verbatim:

'As you know, these days it is very chic, even de rigeur to twin towns having a common interest. Doubtless you know Whitwell-on-the-water, chief fishing port of the Midlands. When we have visited Paris we have noticed that there are many fish in the Seine. It is for that reason that we have thought to twin Whitwell-on-the-water with Paris. We hope you can participate . . . (entente cordiale, mains à travers la mer et tout cela). We would have wished to offer to pay your expenses, but thanks to Mrs Thatcher we are unfortunately too poor . . .'

The day before the twinning ceremony, 13th June 1980, a response was received from the
Mayor's office:

'Monsieur Jacques Chirac, who is appreciative of your attention, has asked me to let you know that it was unfortunately impossible to give a favourable answer to your request.' The note went on to explain that as Paris was officially twinned with Rome, other twinning ceremonies would not be possible. Nevertheless, the ceremonies went ahead and were covered by Central Television News.

Even today, visiting vandals, widely rumoured to be French tourists, appear to occasionally take offence and spray over the lower half of the signs, leading to regular clean-up efforts championed by local Rutland Radio DJ, Rob Persani and supported on occasion by the author.

Les vandales ont encore frappé...

Et après le nettoyage

Rob Persani of Rutland and Stamford Sound with the author and Julie Healey, former landlady of the Noel Arms, Whitwell

Rutland Radio Cruise Day, Summer 2017. (Photo courtesy of Gerry Robinson, the Rutland Belle)

Whitwell Harbour

Whitwell Harbour, or Whitwell Creek as it is sometimes called, is the inlet between the peninsula known as 'Ernie's Point' and Rutland Water North Shore. It is now one of the most popular venues around Rutland Water for tourists and locals alike and be warned, in the height of the season, traffic queues can extend all the way back to the main road – the A606 Oakham to Stamford route. Current attractions are:

- ✓ The Rutland Belle, www.rutlandwatercruises.com, open for afternoon public sailings from April through until the end of October (weekends only in the final month) as well as available for private hire events such as Coffee Cruises, Wedding Parties, Gin Cruises etc.
- ✓ The Harbour Café and the Crafty Fox eateries.
- ✓ Rutland Cycling. https://www.rutlandcycling.com/pages/rutland-cycling-whitwell.aspx
- ✓ Rutland Watersports. https://anglianwaterparks.co.uk/rutland-water-park/watersports Sailing, windsurfing, kayaking, canoeing or stand up paddle boarding.
- ✓ The Aqua Park. https://www.aquaparkrutland.co.uk/

Rutland Water Beach. (Photo courtesy of Anglian Water)

d

Sykes Lane – Monument & Beach

Whitwell Harbour's neighbouring attraction, Sykes Lane, has become incredibly popular over the last few years, especially during hot weather, since the opening of Rutland Water Beach and the same comments about parking at Whitwell Harbour during the height of the season apply here – but more so! The monument, however is somewhat less popular! The 'Great Tower' by Alexander, an Australian sculptor, was commissioned by the International Arts Foundation in 1979. The sculpture, which was cast in London and was then the largest single bronze-cast sculpture in the world, costing £50,000 (over a quarter of a million pounds today), caused outrage at the time. The unveiling ceremony, on 9th October 1980, was boycotted by the local Parish Council at Empingham and missed by the sculptor himself – absent with influenza. The inscription reads, *"The Great Tower By Alexander 1980. Mankind is capable of an awareness that is outside the range of everyday life. My monumental sculptures are created to communicate with that awareness in a way similar to classical music. Just as most symphonies are not intended to be descriptive so these works do not represent figures or objects. Alexander"*

Sykes Lane also hosts the Rutland Water Tourist Information Centre, another in the chain of 'Fox' eateries, Bugtopia (https://anglianwaterparks.co.uk/rutland-water-park/other-activities/bugtopia) Rutland Water Mini-Golf (https://anglianwaterparks.co.uk/rutland-water-park/other_activities/minigolf) and a children's adventure play area.

cc-by-sa/2.0 · Rutland Water dam by Alan Murray-Rust · geograph.org.uk/p/4829467

The Dam

The dam is constructed of clay taken from two separate areas within the reservoir and was built with a stone wave-wall facing into the reservoir to protect the body of the dam itself and a long grass slope on the other side facing roughly north-east towards Empingham village. The dam's vital statistics are: length – two-thirds of a mile (1704 metres or nearly 1200 yards in old money). Height - 40 metres (140 feet). Thickness at base – half a mile (805 metres) narrowing to about 100 metres at the top, which is surmounted by a foot/cycle path with a grass edge. The Draw-Off Tower can be seen at the southern end of the dam through which water is abstracted and then pumped to the Wing Water Treatment Works before being sent on to Anglian Water customers in the areas mentioned in the Rutland Water section of this guide. Between the dam itself and the end of the Hambleton peninsula is the Limnological Tower which contains scientific equipment used to automatically monitor the quality of the water at differing depths. The tower stands in 110 feet of water (the average depth of the reservoir) with the monitoring taking place at six different levels. You may notice one of the results of the work of the tower, with patches of bubbles rising to the surface of the water in areas around the tower. These are caused by oxygen replenishing by injecting compressed air into the water at low levels to aerate it. The exact same principle is used in a home aquarium, in fact.

The Audit Hall, Empingham. (Photo courtesy of Gerry Robinson, The Rutland Belle)

Empingham – A Model Village

Empingham village as we see it today is largely shaped by the work of the Heathcote family, the main landowners from 1729 to 1924. In 1722 it was the largest village in the Normanton Estate which was bought a few years later by Sir Gilbert Heathcote, a successful Merchant Adventurer and Director of the East India Company. At that time, Empingham had houses scattered in traditional fashion around its church and along Main Street. Sir Gilbert's successor John Heathcote, the 2nd Baronet, who was also MP for Grantham, Lincs and Bodmin, Cornwall, worked to increase the Estate following his retirement in 1741 and when it passed to the 3rd Baronet, another Gilbert Heathcote, he decided the time had come to improve the setting and views of Normanton House. Following the popular fashion of making landscape gardens in the Italianate style, the new Baronet decide to move the Normanton villagers to Empingham in order to make his park, which ended up being some 900 acres in total. The new Empingham villagers were housed in rows of thatched cottages, a number of which can still be seen in the village. However, the main work that shaped Empingham was undertaken by the 5th Baronet, Gilbert Henry Heathcote, known as 'The Building Earl'. Taking note of the 1860 Poor Law Commission into rural housing and the dilapidation of Empingham, he built a large workshop and woodyard at Normanton with brickyards at Luffenham and Pilton. Old farms were repaired, with red roof tiles replacing the old thatch, extensions were added and many properties acquired tall

The White Horse, Empingham. (Photo courtesy of Gerry Robinson, The Rutland Belle)

decoratively banded chimneys which can still be seen today. Building of housing with red tiled roofs and tall decorative chimneys for estate workers in the latter part of the 19th century completed the 'look' of Empingham as it appears today. Walking around the village today, you will see the Baron's coronet from when Gilbert Henry was still a Baron. On gaining his Earldom in 1892 subsequent buildings display his Earl's coronet.

The village briefly lent its name to the reservoir, to preserve the 'Rutland' name during the period that Rutland was merged into Leicestershire. The reservoir was then known as 'Empingham Reservoir'. This reverted to Rutland Water following Rutland regaining its independence in 1997.
Empingham is also well known for its association with the Battle of Losecote Field (also known as the Battle of Empingham) which was fought on 12 March 1470, during the Wars of the Roses, near Empingham, to the north-east of the Great North Road (now the A1). The battle, which saw the resounding defeat by the King's forces of the rebel army is popularly attributed its name due to the losing side discarding their jackets displaying the rebel leaders livery so as to avoid capture in the rout that followed. However, it is more likely that the name comes from the Old English phrase *hlose-cot* meaning "pigsty cottage". Losecote also appears as field names in other parishes in Rutland and elsewhere. It is likely that a field at the site of the battle acquired that name, leading to the creative but probably incorrect 'lose coat' etymology which became linked to the battle

Normanton Park – Demolished in 1925 (Photo courtesy of Lost Heritage)

Normanton Park and Village

Early records of Normanton date back to the mid-14th Century when it is estimated that there were around 150 villagers living there. By the early 16th Century, this had dropped to around 90. The manor can be traced back to the 12th Century under the Umfraville family from whom it passed to the Normanvilles, then William de Basing and finally to the Mackworth family in the fifteenth century. The manor was rebuilt by Sir Henry Mackworth in the first half of the seventeenth century and in 1723 the Normanton Estate was sold, along with others to Charles Tryon who, in turn, sold it to Gilbert Heathcote.

1764 is often quoted as the year in which Sir Gilbert Heathcote, the 3rd Baronet, removed the villagers of Normanton to his model village of Empingham, in order to create Normanton Park – in reality the removal took many years, possibly as many as thirty. However, what is known is that the village was totally depopulated by 1796 which was the year when the renowned landscape architect, Humphry Repton visited Normanton and later produced one of his famous 'red books' in which he commented thusly, *"The elegance and magnificence of the house are not at present sufficiently supported by the original size of the park . . . and therefore its extension or enlargement was a very natural object of improvement."* Following that visit, old fences were removed, new approaches and terraces, 'Pleasure Grounds' with walks as well as a kitchen garden and a lake, fed by the Gwash, were all created.

Normanton Park and Normanton House received much praise. In *Beauties of England & Wales (1813)*, J Norris Brewer records that the village was at that time completely depopulated and went on to give a fulsome description of Normanton House itself. Some thirty years later, White's *Directory (1746)* described the *'beautiful Park of about 500 acres, which was considerably enlarged about sixty years ago, when the village was swept away, and its inhabitants removed to Empingham . . . The gardens are modern; and the grounds are tastefully laid out, and command beautiful prospects'*. Normanton House, by then commonly referred to as Normanton Hall, featured in the February 1913 edition of Country Life. However just over ten years later, faced with the immense cost of upkeep, the 2nd Earl of Ancaster decided to sell the Normanton Estate and live at Grimsthorpe Castle. The whole estate was offered for sale in August that year and although lots were bought, the majority failed to reach their reserve value and the mansion and grounds along with a part of Normanton Park were withdrawn from sale. The decision was made to demolish the mansion and auction off its contents and grounds. Much of the stone from the demolished mansion was purchased by Thomas Henry Crumbie and transported to Scraptoft, Leicestershire, and used to build a family home. Later, the house was purchased by a brewery and is now known as The White House, a Wetherspoons in Scraptoft Lane, Leicester! One wonders what Sir Gilbert Heathcote would have thought about that! Today, as mentioned in the boat commentary, all that remains of Normanton House is the former Stable Block – now the Normanton Park Hotel, and the former Gun-Room and Brew House, now Park House.

Normanton Church. (Photo courtesy of Anglian Water)

Normanton Church

Probably the most photographed and certainly the most iconic feature of Rutland Water, St Matthew's Church stands as a permanent memorial to the lost village and park and a reminder of the flooding of the Gwash Valley to create Rutland Water, as well as a tribute to the efforts of the volunteers who saved it from being demolished and drowned. It is believed that the first permanent structure dated back to the end of the fourteenth century and it became much decayed until rebuilt in 1764 by the 3rd Baronet. His successor, the 4th Baronet, commissioned a new porticoed tower said to be modelled on St John's Church, Westminster. Further renovations took place in 1911 with the rebuilding of the chancel and nave and the replacement of the former staircase and gallery with a wide archway on Doric columns. With the decision to flood the Gwash Valley made, the church was deconsecrated by the Bishop of Peterborough in 1970 with all memorials, glass, fittings, graves, gravestones, memorial tablets and the altar slab removed. The little church's future indeed seemed bleak. However, in 1972, the Normanton Tower Trust volunteers campaigned to save the church and this was achieved by raising the internal floor level and building a surrounding bank and causeway for protection. Windows seen at ground level today were originally second storey. In 1983 it became Anglian Water's Rutland Water Museum and today, some events mirror its original use, when it is the venue for Civil Marriage Ceremonies, often in close collaboration with the Rutland Belle.

The Rutland Sailing Club. (Photo courtesy of Rutland Sailing Club)

South Shore – Fishing & Sailing

With very good parking and a host of activities including long walks up to the dam, past Normanton Church, the South Shore has become incredibly popular over recent years and can be very busy in the height of the summer. It also gives access to the rear of the Normanton Park Hotel, the old stable block of Normanton House as described earlier which is also popular for drinks and meals. In short, the attractions on the South Shore include.

- Rutland Sailing School (http://www.rutlandsailingschool.co.uk/) which provides tuition on a wide range of water craft including catamarans and powerboats. Rutland Sailability also operate from here.
- Rutland Water Fishing (https://anglianwaterparks.co.uk/rutland-water-park/fishing) where you can hire tackle and boats to do trout (rainbow and brown) and occasionally predator fishing.
- Rutland Cycling – as per the shop at Whitwell.
- The Four Foxes Café
- The Waterside Café (was L'Oliveto Italian Restaurant but has now reverted to Anglian Water ownership).
- Public Toilet facilities

A short walk from the Normanton Car Park, in one direction lies Normanton Church, described in the previous section, and in the other, the small village of Edith Weston which has a village shop, St Mary the Virgin church and a pub – the Wheatsheaf (http://www.wheatsheafedithweston.co.uk/).

Photo courtesy of Rob Waddington, Owner, Lakeside B&B and Rutland Fly Fishing Adventures

North Shore – Rutland Fly Fishing Adventures (http://rutlandwaterflyfishing.co.uk)

Whilst on the subject of angling, it's worth giving a separate mention to Rutland Fly Fishing Adventures which is an independent local enterprise separate from the fishing offered by Anglian Water in the previous section. Rob Waddington, owner (and also owner of the nearby Lakeside B&B (http://www.thelodgebarnsdale.co.uk)) considers Rutland Water to offer the finest stillwater fly fishing for trout in the UK. The business, which has been running for sixteen years, offers Beginners Courses as well as Group Events, Guiding Services and Presentations. In addition to Trout, Rob also offers Pike and Zander fishing too.

Lakeside B&B

Photo courtesy of Geoff Harries

South Arm – Nature Reserve

Rutland Water is shaped like a horse-shoe lying on its side which is fitting as the County emblem is a golden horseshoe being mobbed by acorns – a reference to the the long-established practice that peers of the realm forfeit a horseshoe to the Lord of the Manor of Oakham on their first visit to the town. There are well over two hundred today on the walls of Oakham Castle. The South Arm runs from the tiny village of Egleton at its western end and is flanked by the south shore and Hambleton peninsula.
The South Arm is principally of interest because of its role as a nature reserve. It has been enhanced by the addition of new lagoons and a wide range of waterfowl and other birds, including the famous Osprey, can readily be seen here. The Anglian Birdwatching Centre (featured annually at the Bird Fair) lies just south of Egleton. The reserve itself is managed by the Leicestershire & Rutland Wildlife Trust in partnership with Anglian Water, providing a wildfowl sanctuary for over 25,000 waterfowl. It's also an SSI (Site of Special Scientific Interest), an ESPA (European Special Protection Area) and a RAMSAR site (Ramsar Convention on Wetlands of International Importance especially as Waterfowl Habitat, named after the city of Ramsar in Iran, where the Convention was signed in 1971).

Photo courtesy of Rod Baker

The Reserve was originally created in the 1970s alongside the construction of the reservoir itself and following expansions, now covers 1000 acres of shoreline and shallow lagoons along 9 miles at the western end of Rutland Water.

Aside from the Anglian Water Birdwatching Centre at Egleton which contains environmental displays and a viewing gallery, visitors can also visit the Lyndon Visitor Centre which is some way further along the south shore, heading east between the villages of Manton and Edith Weston. Lyndon contains the Wildlife and Weather Exhibition and both centres have a Wildlife Trust shop.

For those interested in conservation there are volunteer opportunities at both sites.

The Old Post Office, Hambleton. (Photo courtesy of Kate Jewell, Geograph)

Hambleton Peninsula and The Hambletons

What is now a peninsula was once the centre of the extended parish of Hambleton. Now just the main village, centred around the parish church, survives above the waters of the reservoir. Its outlying hamlets once straggled down the south side of Hambleton Hill, with Nether Hambleton lowest and closest to the River Gwash. The road from Egleton then ran westwards, into Nether Hambleton where it branched left to carry on up through Middle Hambleton to Upper Hambleton and right to Lyndon, crossing the Manton to Edith Weston road. In Upper Hambleton, the road branched again, left to join the main Oakham to Stamford road and right to Normanton, Whitwell and Empingham. Essentially, as the Rutland Belle passes Old Hall on the starboard side and the high point known as Browns Island today portside, the boat is sailing over the sites of Nether and Middle Hambleton. Hambleton, overall, dates back to before 1066, being part of the dower of Saxon queens including Edward the Confessor's wife, Edith of Wessex, after whom Edith Weston is named. By the time of the Domesday Book, Hambleton and its associated lands contained three churches and seven hamlets. Under the powerful Norman family, the Umfravilles, the manor was divided into Great and Little Hambleton, the latter passing to the Flore family in 1412. Their Oakham townhouse still remains as Flore's House on Oakham High Street.

Burley on the Hill showing the Cour D'Honneur and Holy Cross Church. (Photo courtesy of Richard Adams)

The North Arm and Burley-on-the-Hill

The Rutland Belle is unique in that it has the freedom to tour the whole reservoir, which is especially important on Osprey Cruises where the Captain can take the boat to wherever the birds are fishing. Sometimes this includes heading up the North Arm, not usually included in our regular cruises. You will see, on the starboard side, as we near the end of the arm, an imposing 'big house', Burley House. Before Rutland Water became the main feature for visitors to Rutland, Burley House held that place. Burley takes its name from the Old English *burh* 'fortified manor' plus *leah* 'woodland clearing'. The Domesday survey recorded that Burley had 38 villagers and smallholders, working for the lord of the manor, Geoffrey, 'Gilbert of Ghent's man'. The manor stayed in that family for some 200 years until in the late 1200s the heiress, Alice, married Sir Nicholas de Segrave. 300 years later, the War of the Roses found the manor in the hands of the Sapcote family who were Yorkists. Alabaster effigies, thought to represent Sir Thomas Sapcote and his wife, Joan, can be seen in Burley Church (the Church of the Holy Cross) today. The Sapcote line died out in 1550, the manor passing to the Haringtons, the youngest son of Sir James Harington having married Frances Sapcote. The Haringtons were one of the largest land owners in England and Sir James made his main residence at Exton where he completely rebuilt that manor house. Burley next featured nationally in 1603 when King James I of England (King James VI of Scotland) began his progress south to claim his crown following the death of Queen Elizabeth I. The king stayed at Belvoir Castle, Leicestershire, on Maundy Thursday, Burley House on Good Friday and then on Easter Saturday, following a morning hunt in Exton Park, went on to Stamford to stay with the Cecil family at Burghley House. Following the death of Sir John Harington in 1613, his son, also John, encumbered with debts and in poor health himself drew up wills to enable his heirs to sell land to discharge those debts and died of smallpox just nine days later. Exton Estate passed eventually to the 2nd Viscount Campden, Sir Edward Noel, with Burley being bought by the king's favourite, George Villiers. *(The 4th Viscount Campden was made Earl of Gainsborough and the Noels still live at Exton today).* George Villiers, who was made 1st Duke of Buckingham, built the mansion preceding the one seen today and although contemporary writers describe the house as 'improved' there are suggestions that it was, in fact, entirely rebuilt. Buckingham is also remembered locally for his gift of the Rutland dwarf, Jeffrey Hudson, to Queen Henrietta, the wife of King Charles I. A cottage traditionally said to be Hudson's can still be seen in Oakham today opposite what used to be the White Lion pub, now a commercial property. During the Civil War, Rutland fell into the hands of the parliamentarians and Sir Edward Harington, having seized Oakham Castle with its magazine of arms, assisted Lord Grey of Groby, Leicestershire, in the occupation of Burley House. The mansion became the headquarters of the Rutland County Committee, governing the county in the name of Parliament. Villiers, a royalist, had his estates officially confiscated, and Burley became the property of Parliament. In 1645-46 and in defiance of orders from Parliament, Burley House 'was '. . . *utterly consumed by fire so that at present there remains nothing but certain ruinous parts and pieces of the walls'.*

Restoration of the monarchy in 1661 meant the restitution of confiscated land and property and so Burley-on-the-Hill once again passed to Buckingham. However the 2nd Duke took little interest on it and after he died it was bought by Daniel Finch, 2nd Earl of Nottingham who would build the mansion that we see today. The mansion was finally completed around 1710. Nearly a hundred years later, the 4th Earl of Nottingham, having made several improvements to the estate, decided to bring in Humphrey Repton to review the land. Repton visited in 1795 and made several recommendations, not all of which were carried out, and during that period John Nash, the famous architect, was brought in to design Home Farmhouse, still standing and in private hands as are the remaining Home Farm buildings.

By the turn of the century, the mansion was in the hands of a commoner, although related to the Finches – Alan George Finch who rented it out to a well-known politician, Frederick Guest, cousin of Winston Churchill who was staying at the house when it caught fire on 9th August 1908, destroying most of the interior of the western half of the mansion. Burley went on to be used as a hospital for officers recovering from trench warfare, as portrayed in Downton Abbey. The last private owner of the mansion was Evan (Joss) Hanbury who still lives near Burley and who sold the estate to Asil Nadir, of Polly Peck infamy, and then, following the Asil Nadir bankruptcy worked with architect, Kit Martin, to convert the mansion and its outbuildings into a series of luxury houses and apartments all of which are now in private hands.

Photo courtesy of Rod Baker

The Rutland Ospreys

If Rutland Water has become the iconic feature at the heart of Rutland and Normanton Church the most iconic building, then Rutland's most iconic inhabitant has to be the Rutland Osprey.

1978, the year that Rutland Water became operational, was also the first time that an Osprey, probably on its way back to its breeding grounds in Scotland, was sighted. Osprey sightings were extremely rare and the sighting on 4th May caused huge excitement, bearing in mind that from being commonplace in the seventeenth century, Ospreys were most likely extinct in Britain by the early twentieth century. By the mid-1950s however, a pair began to breed at Loch Garten and with the help of dedicated nest protectors the colony grew until by the late seventies approximately 40 Ospreys were migrating north from Africa each spring and returning to the African wetlands at the end of each autumn. As the Scottish population grew, and the habitats surrounding Rutland Water improved, the number of Osprey visits increased until in 1994 a female stayed for the whole summer, raising hopes that they might breed here. The LRWT built artificial Osprey platforms to encourage this and by the mid-1990s a plan to translocate a number of young birds from Scotland over a six-year period was approved. This was successfully achieved but an even bigger milestone was met when in 1999 the first of the translocated birds returned to Rutland Water for the summer.

Osprey nest with Burley House in distance. (Photo courtesy of John Wright)

2001 saw the first Rutland Osprey chick to be born. The Ospreys had returned to England!

In 2019, the Rutland Osprey Project celebrated the hatching of the 150th Osprey chick at Rutland Water and have a total of nine breeding pairs. Topically, it is understood that the wood from the original ancient Oak used for the site of the first Osprey nest, which is now no longer needed, is being used in the repairs of Notre Dame.

The Rutland Belle runs early morning and evening Osprey Cruises from May through to August every year. These are run by the Rutland Osprey Project who provide spotters and commentators who are able to talk not only about the Osprey but other birds of interest. The Rutland Belle has the freedom to cruise the whole reservoir meaning that we can reach the western extremities of the South Arm where the Osprey nesting grounds are as well as follow them the length and breadth of Rutland Water to watch them fish. These cruises are incredibly popular and early booking is recommended.

To book an Osprey Cruise visit the Rutland Osprey Project: https://www.lrwt.org.uk/osprey-cruises

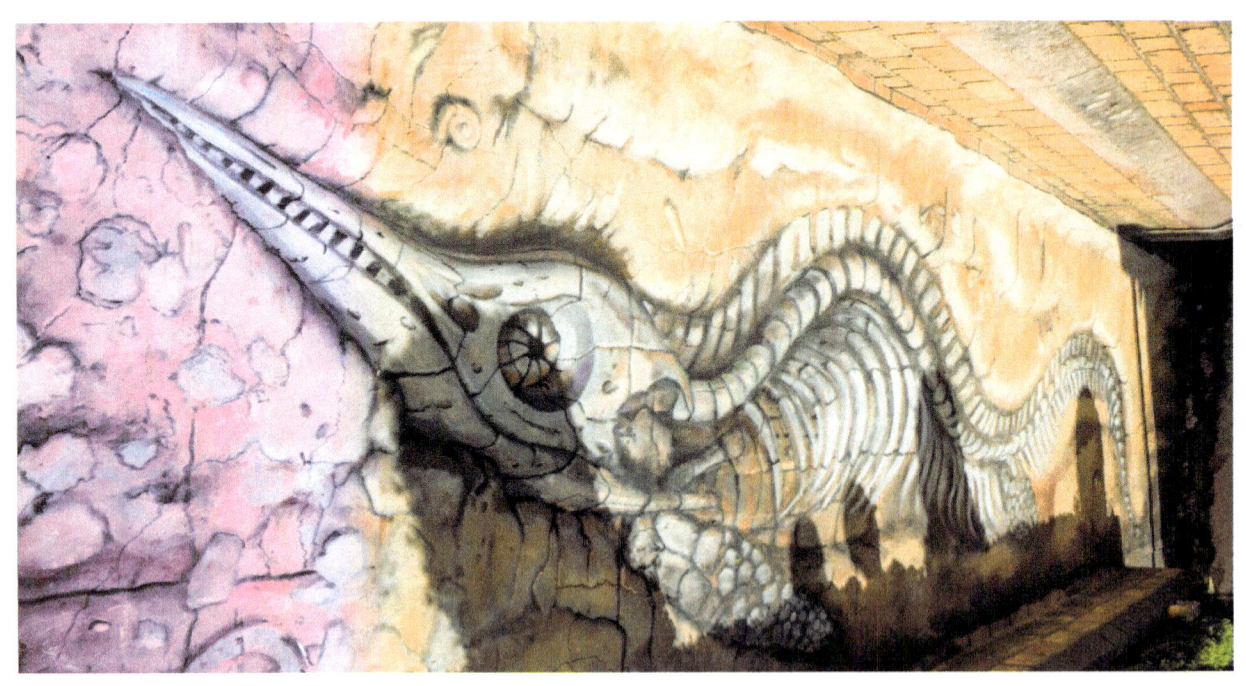

Local Pavement Chalk Artist, Julian Beever recreated the Rutland Sea Dragon in Mill Street, Oakham. May 2022

The Rutland Sea Dragon – Ancient History is brought to life!

In January 2022 prehistoric fever gripped Rutland when the news broke that a fossilised ichthyosaur had been discovered at Rutland Water. Even more remarkable and a fascinating insight into how this part of the world has changed over millennia was the fact that ichthyosaurs were ocean-going reptiles from the time of the dinosaurs and Rutland is about as far from the ocean as you can get in England – about forty miles as the crow flies to the closest point of The Wash. However, 200 million years ago it was under a shallow ocean.

The discovery was actually made in February 2021 during landscaping work at Rutland Water Nature Reserve and left in place until the water levels lowered again late in the summer of 2021 when the remains were excavated by a team of palaeontologists. The whole excavation being shrouded in secrecy to prevent fossil-hunting amongst other issues.

At the time of writing, the fossilised ichthyosaur is at an industrial unit in Shropshire where it is planned to be fully uncovered and with the hope that with the backing of Rutland's MP, Alicia Kearns, it will return to Rutland at some point in the future to be permanently displayed at Rutland Water.

'Rutty' The Rutland Dinosaur on display at Leicester's New Walk Museum – Photo courtesy of Leicester Mercury

Rutlanders have good reason to be jealous of the provenance of the Sea Dragon going forward. In June 1968 the fossilised remains of a Cetiosaurus Oxoniensis was discovered at the Williamson Cliff Quarry near Great Casterton which turned out to be the most complete specimen of its kind.

Cetiosauruses belonged to the Sauropod group (more commonly known as Brontosaurs) and this particular specimen is believed to be 168 million years old.

However, Rutty, as he is nicknamed, did not stay in Rutland but rather has been on display at Leicester's New Walk Museum since 1985

In 2021, more ancient history came to light in a remote corner of a Rutland farmer's film with the discover of the 'Rutland Mosaic' – a three panel mosaic depicting events from the Trojan War in which the Greek hero, Achilles, fights, kills and ransoms the body of Hector, prince of the Trojans.

With an ever-increasing number of tourists choosing to visit Rutland, it's hoped that Rutland Water will one day host a visitor centre fit to host and display these fascinating glimpses into Rutland's past.

Barnsdale Gardens, Barnsdale Avenue, Exton – Photo courtesy of Nick Hamilton, Barnsdale Gardens

Barnsdale Gardens – It's In The Genes

There is actually no village or parish of Barnsdale in Rutland. Barnsdale Gardens, along with Barnsdale Lodge Hotel and Rutland Hall Hotel (until recently Barnsdale Hall Hotel) all lie within the parish of Exton and are neighboured by Burley parish. One of the first written references to Barnsdale was in 1283 when Bernard de Brus of Exton donated *'the income from the church of Exton 'and all the Tithes of Hay, which in his Park of Bernardyshill, or elsewhere they have been accustomed to receive'* to the monks and church of St Andrew, Northampton. Bernards Hill or Barnsdale was in fact a medieval hunting park in Exton parish and near to the border with Whitwell parish, one of ten such parks in medieval Rutland.

Geoff Hamilton *(15 August 1936 – 4 August 1996),* an English author, broadcaster and gardener was probably best known as the presenter of Gardeners World in the 1980s and 90s. After graduating from agricultural college in Writtle, Essex, he worked as a nurseryman and self-employed landscape gardener, before opening his own garden centre on the outskirts of Kettering. As a full-time journalist and editor of Practical Gardening magazine, he used his position to inform the public about the joys and benefits of organic gardening.

Weddings at Barnsdale Gardens – Photo courtesy of Steve Hamilton, Hamilton Photography

He began developing the garden, on Exton Avenue, in 1985, from what was then a ploughed field belonging to the Exton Estate and today it covers eight acres including thirty-eight gardens. From 1979 until his death, Geoff Hamilton presented Gardener's World and in 1985 was responsible for moving the show to Barnsdale Gardens. He was a well-known and popular local character, and was involved in the 'Whitwell Twinning Project' along with the then landlord of the Noel Arms, Sam Healey, as described earlier in this book.

Today, Geoff's legacy has passed on to his son, Nick Hamilton and Barnsdale Gardens, just one mile away from the Rutland Belle's mooring at Whitwell, remains a very popular, coach friendly, Rutland tourist attraction with its large range of gardens, tea room, shop and nursery. For full details visit:

https://barnsdalegardens.co.uk/index.html

Nick Hamilton's own book – The Right Genes – available from Amazon in both paperback and Kindle formats and also available in the Barnsdale Gardens shop is well worth reading as part of a visit to this area of Rutland.

Engine Shed – Photo Courtesy of Rocks By Rail, Living Ironstone Museum, Cottesmore (https://www.rocks-by-rail.org/)

Rocks By Rail – The Living Ironstone Museum

Iron ore has been worked in Rutland since Roman Times with smelting on a large scale known to have been carried out at Thistleton, Clipsham, Pickworth and Harringworth. The Domesday Book records three Ferraria (forges) at Castle Bytham – just over the Rutland border. Iron ore extraction continued through the Middle Ages finally reaching its peak in the seventeenth century when Rockingham Castle, near Rutland, was built on the 'Lincoln Edge' to safeguard the Royal Forges. Production eased off during the Industrial Revolution to be replaced by ironworks in coal-producing areas however once these began to be worked out, the advancement of the rail network meant that ore dug in non coal-producing areas could be easily transported for smelting.

The Gainsborough Estate (Exton Hall) signed a lease for land within the Cottesmore parish with Sheepbridge Coal & Iron Company in November 1880 with iron ore production commencing in 1882. By the 20th Century iron ore working had transformed the face of Rutland in this area. To quote from a 1959 guide to Cottesmore (about five miles north of Whitwell Harbour), *"The ironstone mining has very much altered the face of the country round Cottesmore in recent years. This opencast mining which surrounds the village on three sides, North, south and west has lowered the level of the fields by some ten to twenty feet, cut through the beautiful Exton woods and swept away old field paths, springs and other natural landmarks..... The road to Market Overton now appears to run on a causeway, since the fields on both sides have been excavated and put back at a lower level and some farms and barns appear to have been built on small islands."*

Photo Courtesy of Rocks By Rail (https://www.rocks-by-rail.org/)

The origins of the Rocks by Rail Museum itself lie with the construction of a mineral branch off the Syston to Peterborough line by the Midland Railway to serve the local quarries. This new line started just north of Ashwell Station running for three miles to a railhead near Cottesmore on the Ashwell Road. This railhead is the current location of Rocks by Rail. It was completed in 1882 to serve the Cottesmore quarries but then used by the new quarries at Burley, after World War One and Exton Park, after World War Two.

Rocks by Rail – The Living Ironstone Museum covers nineteen acres of reclaimed quarry, railway tracks and nature trails. In addition to the nature trails, Rocks by Rail offers the chance to take a train ride or even drive a classic locomotive on their 'Driver For A Fiver!' days as well as visiting the exhibition centre and workshop before finishing off the day in a 1960s style café (but without the limp cheese sandwiches remembered in the old days of British Rail).

Rocks by Rail can be found roughly halfway down Cottesmore Road between Cottesmore and Ashwell (postcode LE15 7FF), contactable on 07873 721941. Website: https://www.rocks-by-rail.org/

All Aboard a Rocks By Rail Loco!

Photo courtesy of Max Ludgate of Rutland Drone (Instagram - @rutland_drone)

2021 – New Year - New Look

Like the rest of the country, in 2020 Rutland Water Cruises were heavily impacted by the Covid crisis. Crew were furloughed and the Season Opening which usually takes place at Easter was delayed until July. The bookings calendar turned purple as coach company after coach company cancelled their bookings and weddings were put back one year and in some cases two. We finally opened on 4th July 2021 with the strictest of Covid precautions in place. Plastic screens were fitted to the Ticket Office, passengers were required to wear facemasks, boarding was via spaced queues, table service on the boat replaced visits to the bar and like every other leisure industry we became obsessed with wiping everything down between trips. And yet, probably due to the fact that nobody was going abroad, we were surprisingly busy during the height of the season and Rutland Water became a magnet for those cooped up in the surrounding cities of Leicester, Nottingham and Peterborough.

As Robert Walter postulated in his 1879 Journal 'The Laws of Health', *"Sunlight is the best disinfectant"* and perhaps this contributed to a long-discussed idea of replacing the existing wheelhouse with a taller one, sitting further forward thus giving yet more seating area outside as well as other operational benefits and unintentionally giving the Belle something of a tugboat appearance but a more stately profile.

The New Wheelhouse arrives with crane to lift into place - Photo by Gerry Robinson, Rutland Belle

Once the Season had closed, work got under way and the new wheelhouse, was delivered to the Wymondham workshop for fitting out. That work went on through the winter months and by the new year we were ready to install the new wheelhouse forward of the existing one where it snuggled securely into an existing gap that had once been the location of a large sliding sunroof over the forrard saloon. New railings and a move forward of the two lifeboat capsules have now completed the new look and today proud passengers can, in addition to enjoying the views from the upper deck, now sit on a raised 'Captain's Deck' on the same level as the new wheelhouse.

Trends continually change and for sure more changes will come to the boat which has now spent nearly thirty-seven years on the water but the Belle's core purpose will never change – bringing enjoyment of Rutland Water's many attractions to thousands of visitors every year.

Rutland Belle pre 2021, with Wedding Cruise bunting and a gaff-rigged yacht in the background (Matt Broadhead)

The Rutland Belle, Class V Passenger Vessel

The Rutland Belle is a Class V Passenger Vessel, 62 feet long from bow to stern and 15.5 feet abeam, it displaces 32 tonnes and draws 3.5 feet of water. The boat can carry a maximum of 110 people with up to 70 in the aft and forward saloons. It boasts a galley and head (bar and toilet) and is equipped with a 250 kg SWL hydraulic lift for wheelchairs or passengers unable to use the steps down into the boat. Minimum crewing requirement is the Skipper - a licensed Boatmaster and a crewman.

In 2020, as previously mentioned, the boat underwent an extensive refit, moving the wheelhouse forward and into a more elevated position and freeing up more upper deck space.

During the early 1980s Trevor and Joan Broadhead, the original owners, were running a hire-boat and trip-boat business (Charnwood Marine Ltd) on the River Soar near Leicester. Noticing an article in the Leicester Mercury by Anglian Water, inviting interested parties to tender to run a trip-boat on Rutland Water from April 1985, they prepared a proposal to construct a new, purpose-built vessel to commence operation in the summer of 1985. Their proposal was accepted and the Rutland Belle was built at Ollerton, near Newark and launched at the end of that season, early in November 1985. Engine enthusiasts will be interested to learn that the Belle is powered by a 1947 Gardner 5LW engine originally from a generator set used to supply auxiliary power to the Royal Train.

As a British Merchantmen, the Rutland Belle flies the Red Ensign when in passage.

Photo Courtesy of Kathy Robinson

Multum in Parvo - Rutland In Brief

There was much excitement and some reservations on the 1st April 1997 when Rutland regained its independence becoming a County and a Unitary Authority in its own right. Rutland County Council became responsible for almost all local services in Rutland, with the exception of the Leicestershire Fire and Rescue Service and Leicestershire Police. Rutland regained a separate lieutenancy and shrievalty, with the current incumbents at the time of writing being Doctor Sarah Furness, Lord Lieutenant and Geoff Thompson, High Sheriff and thus also regained status as a ceremonial county.

For the previous twenty-three years, Rutland had been a district of Leicestershire. But of course, Rutland's history goes back much further than 1974. It was first mentioned as a separate county in 1159 although right up to the 14th Century it was referred to as the *Soke* of Rutland – Soke being an Old English word generally implying 'Jurisdiction'. One of the first useages of the word 'Rutland' is thought to be in the Will of Edward The Confessor where it's referred to as 'Roteland' and in the Domesday Book it's referred to as *'The Kiny's Soc of Roteland'*, Soc being another spelling of Soke.

The Domesday Book also recorded the north-western part of Rutland as being a detached part of Nottinghamshire and the south-eastern part as *wapentake* (Danelaw equivalent of the Anglo-Saxon Hundred) of Wicelsea in Northamptonshire.

By the 19th Century Rutland had been divided into the hundreds of Alstoe, East Rutland, Martinsley, Oakham and Wrandike. Under the Local Government Act 1894 the previous rural sanitary districts were partitioned along county boundaries to form rural districts then came the "East Midlands General Review Area" of the 1958–67 Local Government Commission for England. Initial recommendations would have seen Rutland split, with Ketton Rural District going along with Stamford to a new administrative county of Cambridgeshire, and the western part added to Leicestershire. However the final proposal was that Rutland become a single rural district within the administrative county of Leicestershire. Under the Local Government Act 1972, which took effect on 1st April 1974,https://en.wikipedia.org/wiki/Rutland - cite_note-10 Rutland became a non-metropolitan district of Leicestershire. Although it was originally proposed that Rutland be merged with what is now Melton Borough as Rutland did not meet the population requirement of at least 40,000 the revised proposals allowed Rutland to be exempt from this.

As the visitor will easily observe, Rutland is a largely agricultural county but also has significant other large employers including the Landsend European Distribution Centre, Ketton Cement, Rutland Plastics, the MoD (Kendrew Barracks (previously RAF Cottemore) and St George's Barracks (previously RAF North Luffenham), two large public schools – Oakham and Uppingham and HM Prison Stocken. Rutland, undoubtedly due to Rutland Water has a flourishing and growing tourism industry with Rutland's de facto Tourist Office, Discover Rutland publishing figures for 2020 (a year when figures were significantly depressed due to Covid) showing economic impact of tourism in Rutland: £63.77 million *(down 55% on 2019)*, visitor numbers in Rutland: 818,000 *(down 56% on 2019)* and employment supported by tourism in Rutland (full time equivalent): 857 *(down 52% on 2019)*. All of these indicators are back up again at the time of writing and by visiting you are a part of that.

Welcome to Rutland and do come again!

Acknowledgements

First and foremost, my thanks go to my two proof-readers, Tim Clough, former Curator of the Rutland County Museum and a huge source of knowledge on Rutland history and my daughter, Kirsty, an international English teacher and like Tim, an expert at spotting superfluous commas!
Then to everyone involved in creating the weighty but well worth reading tome – *The Heritage of Rutland Water*. This is a marvellous reference for anyone interested in the history and geography of Rutland and although no longer in print is available as a pdf copy online via www.rutlandhistory.org.
Finally, to the local people that I've talked to over my twenty years in Rutland, from Meadows Limousine drivers to Rutland Belle crew and passengers, the Rutland Osprey team and kind people at Anglian Water. Journeys, whether long airport transfers or 45-minute cruises invite conversations and the opportunity to learn a little more about this part of the world. I recommend it!

Book design edited by Hannah Reid (www.hannahreiddesign.myportfolio.com)

Photo Credits

Book Cover	Max Ludgate of Rutland Drone (Instagram - @rutland_drone)
Safety Announcements	Captain Matt Broadhead, The Rutland Belle (www.rutlandwatercruises.com)
Rutland Water	Map - Discover Rutland (www.discoverrutland.co.uk)
Rutland Water	Aerial Photo - Rob Waddington, owner of Lakeside B&B (http://www.thelodgebarnsdale.co.uk)
Whitwell	Twinning - Julie Healey, ex Landlady, The Noel Arms, Whitwell
Whitwell	Twinning - Julie Healey, ex Landlady, The Noel Arms, Whitwell
Whitwell	The Noel - Gerry Robinson, The Rutland Belle (www.rutlandwatercruises.com)
Whitwell	Whitwell Sign – Rutland Radio (Now Rutland & Stamford Sound)
Whitwell Harbour	Gerry Robinson, The Rutland Belle (www.rutlandwatercruises.com)
Sykes Lane	Anglian Water (www.anglianwater.co.uk)
The Dam	Alan Murray-Rust (www.geograph.org.uk)
Empingham	Audit Hall - Gerry Robinson, The Rutland Belle (www.rutlandwatercruises.com)
Empingham	The White Horse - Gerry Robinson, The Rutland Belle (www.rutlandwatercruises.com)
Normanton Park	Matthew Beckett, Lost Heritage (www.lostheritage.co.uk)
Normanton Park	Lithograph - Rutland Local History & Record Society (www.rutlandhistory.org)
Normanton Church	Anglian Water (www.anglianwater.co.uk)
South Shore	Rutland Sailing Club (www.rutlandsailingclub.co.uk) and Rutland Sailing School

North Shore	Rob Waddington, owner of Rutland Fly Fishing Adventures (www.rutlandwaterflyfishing.co.uk)
North Shore	Lakeside B & B - Rob Waddington, owner of Lakeside B&B (www.thelodgebarnsdale.co.uk)
South Arm	Osprey Catch - Geoff Harries
South Arm	Firecrest – Rod Baker
Hambleton	Kate Jewell (www.geograph.org.uk)
Burley on the Hill	Richard Adams
Rutland Ospreys	Osprey Catch - Rod Baker
Rutland Ospreys	Osprey Nest - John Wright formerly of the Rutland Water Nature Reserve (www.rutlandwater.org.uk)
The Rutland Sea Dragon	Pavement Art - The Mill Street Traders Action Group of Oakham (MSTAG), 3D Artist Julian Beever, (https://www.julianbeever.net/), Photographer Elli Dean, (https://www.ellideanphotography.co.uk/)
The Rutland Sea Dragon	'Rutty' – The Leicester Mercury, (https://www.leicestermercury.co.uk/)
Barnsdale Gardens	Map – Nick Hamilton, Barnsdale Gardens, (https://barnsdalegardens.co.uk/)
Barnsdale Gardens	Pavilion – Steve Hamilton, Hamilton Photography
Rocks By Rail	Loco Shed – Rocks By Rail Living Ironstone Museum (https://www.rocks-by-rail.org/)
Rocks By Rail	Woolsthorpe Workshop - Rocks By Rail Living Ironstone Museum
New Year – New Look	Max Ludgate of Rutland Drone (Instagram - @rutland_drone)
New Year – New Look	Crane and New Wheelhouse - Gerry Robinson, The Rutland Belle (www.rutlandwatercruises.com)
The Rutland Belle	Boat with yacht in background - Captain Matt Broadhead, The Rutland Belle
Multum in Parvo	Kathy Robinson

Printed in Great Britain
by Amazon